## Rescues in Focus
# Animal Rescues
by Mark L. Lewis

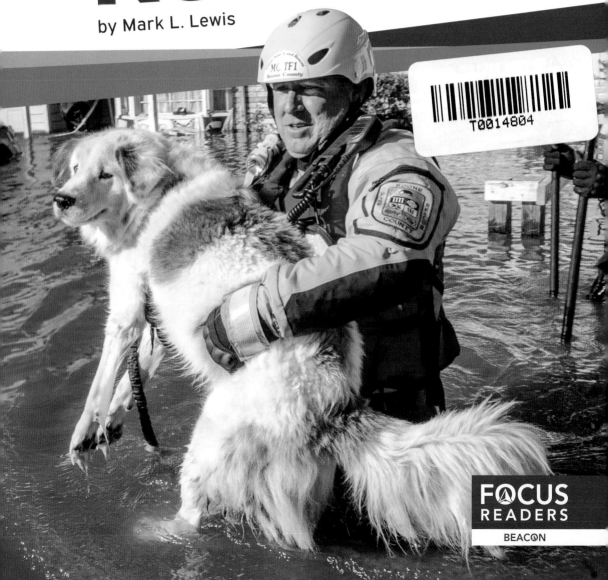

T0014804

FOCUS READERS

BEACON

# www.focusreaders.com

Focus Readers is distributed by North Star Editions:
sales@northstareditions.com | 888-417-0195

Produced for Focus Readers by Red Line Editorial.

Photographs ©: Jocelyn Augustino/FEMA, cover, 1; NOAA, 4; Office of Governor Jindal/Louisiana Governor's Office of Homeland Security & Emergency Management, 7, 29; Zuma Press, Inc./Alamy, 9; songpholt/Shutterstock Images, 10; Robin Loznak/Daily Inter Lake/AP Images, 13; Staff Sgt. Mary Junell/US Army/Defense Visual Information Distribution Service, 15; Ricardo Moraes/AP Images, 17; Octavio Hoyos/Shutterstock Images, 18–19; Dita Alangkara/AP Images, 20; Gareth Fuller/PA Wire URN:29097558/Press Association/AP Images, 23; John Lovretta/The Hawk Eye/AP Images, 25; Alain Pitton/NurPhoto/Getty Images, 26 (left); Dave Saville/FEMA News Photo/FEMA, 26 (right)

**Library of Congress Cataloging-in-Publication Data**
Names: Lewis, Mark L., 1991- author.
Title: Animal rescues / Mark L. Lewis.
Description: Lake Elmo, MN : Focus Readers, [2020] | Series: Rescues in focus |
  Includes bibliographical references and index.
Identifiers: LCCN 2019006121 (print) | LCCN 2019008941 (ebook) | ISBN
  9781641859776 (pdf) | ISBN 9781641859080 (ebook) | ISBN 9781641857703
  (hardcover) | ISBN 9781641858397 (pbk.)
Subjects: LCSH: Animal rescue--Juvenile literature. | Wildlife
  rescue--Juvenile literature.
Classification: LCC HV4708 (ebook) | LCC HV4708 .L49 2020 (print) | DDC
  636.08/32--dc23
LC record available at https://lccn.loc.gov/2019006121

Printed in the United States of America
Mankato, MN
May, 2019

# About the Author

Mark L. Lewis lives in Minnesota but has traveled all over the world. He loves writing books for young readers.

# Table of Contents

# Chapter 1

# Gulf Oil Spill

In 2010, an **oil rig** exploded in the Gulf of Mexico. The explosion caused a huge oil spill. Millions of gallons of oil gushed into the sea. The oil polluted the water and shores. It affected many animals.

**Oil floats on the water's surface in the Gulf of Mexico.**

The oil caused heart problems in fish. Sea turtles had trouble laying eggs. And some animals had trouble escaping the spill. One was the brown pelican.

Pelicans dive into the ocean for food. But oil covered the pelicans when they entered the water. The oil made it hard for them to fly.

**Did You Know?**

Workers can use up to 300 gallons (1,100 L) of water to clean one pelican.

 **The brown pelican is Louisiana's state bird.**

Rescue workers paddled in kayaks. They traveled to nearby islands. They found animals that were completely covered in oil. The rescuers took the animals to animal shelters.

At the animal shelters, rescuers washed the animals with vegetable oil. The vegetable oil broke down the oil from the oil spill. Then the workers used dish soap to clean the animals.

Afterward, workers brought the animals to wildlife **refuges**. These refuges were not the animals' original homes. But the animals would be kept safe from the oil spill. Rescuers saved more than 350 brown pelicans.

 Rescue workers use vegetable oil to break down the oil on a brown pelican.

# Chapter 2

# Becoming a Rescuer

People take different paths to become animal rescuers. Some people work as **volunteers**. Others rescue animals as part of their job. For example, firefighters and soldiers often rescue animals.

**If the animals have no owner, firefighters sometimes adopt the animals they rescue.**

Other animal rescuers work for animal **welfare** groups. These groups help animals in need.

Many rescuers take classes to gain skills for working with animals. Some classes teach rescuers how to tell if an animal is hurt. Some teach **CPR** for hurt animals. Other courses teach animal **behavior**.

Did You Know?

Scared animals might try to bite. Rescuers need to be careful.

 **An animal control officer shows how to perform CPR on a dog.**

Rescuers also learn skills for moving large, injured animals. They might practice using a rescue glide.

A rescue glide is like a large sled. Rescuers roll the animal onto the rescue glide. Then, they drag the animal to safety.

Animal rescuers also train for natural disasters and emergencies. For instance, rescuers practice using ropes and **harnesses**. These tools let rescuers work safely in flooded areas.

Human activity often puts wild animals in danger. Wildlife **conservation** groups help with

> **A member of the US National Guard hooks himself to a rope during flood rescue training.**

these rescues. For example, one group in India protects endangered falcons. Members of the group help keep the falcons safe from hunters.

Wildlife conservation groups also protect areas where animals live. These groups try to help animals before there is an emergency.

Some animal rescuers have more advanced training than others. For example, rescue teams often include a **veterinarian**. Vets study

**Did You Know?**

In 2016, a police officer rescued a bald eagle. A car had hit the eagle on a highway.

 **A veterinarian treats a rescued penguin in Brazil.**

for four years after finishing college. They learn about the science of animal bodies. They help animals that are hurt the worst.

# Earthquake in Mexico

A strong earthquake hit Mexico in 2017. The earthquake destroyed many buildings. In Mexico City, a medical lab caved in. Animals were trapped under the rubble. They needed help. Workers discovered the animals while clearing away debris. They rescued 40 rabbits and 13 rats.

The earthquake also destroyed many people's homes. Those people needed shelter. But they also had pets. So, the city's mayor allowed people to bring their pets with them to the shelters.

Dogs often help with rescue efforts after earthquakes..

# Chapter 3

# On the Job

Rescuers jump into action after an emergency. For example, a call comes in about a house fire. Rescuers learn that the family had to leave without their pet. The team prepares its equipment.

 **A veterinarian prepares equipment before a rescue effort. He is helping rescue apes in Southeast Asia.**

The tools may include a leash, headlamp, and helmet. Rescuers might also include a crate to hold the animal.

Sometimes an animal is trapped in a building. In that case, rescuers may use bolt cutters to break locks. And they may use a **ram** to break down a door.

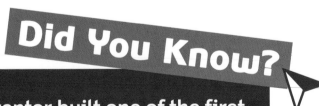

Did You Know?

In 1991, an inventor built one of the first breathing masks meant for animals.

 **A firefighter shows how to use a breathing mask on a dog.**

During a fire, an animal may inhale too much smoke. Rescuers put a mask over the animal's nose. The mask helps the animal breathe.

Rescuers need certain tools for different problems. For example, rescuers may need boats for floods. They may also need suits to stay dry. After an earthquake, rescuers use shovels to remove rubble. During a wildfire, rescuers may need suits that will not catch on fire. If an animal is hard to reach, rescuers may use a catch pole.

After a disaster, animals may be afraid. Scared animals sometimes think rescuers are trying to hurt

 **An animal control officer uses a catch pole to rescue a raccoon.**

them. The animals try to defend themselves. For this reason, rescuers wear thick gloves. Gloves protect their hands if animals bite.

Rescuers may bring pets to an animal shelter. But rescuers take wild animals to a wildlife refuge.

headlamp

helmet

animal crate

dry suit

boat

net

Wildlife refuges are more like the animals' original home. When an animal gets better, workers let it go back into the wild.

Welfare groups help with rescues. They provide people and money.

Firefighters, police officers, and soldiers may also help. These workers need to balance rescuing people with rescuing animals. But animals are important. Pets matter a lot to many people. And wild animals are needed on Earth. Animal rescuers help keep these animals safe.

**Did You Know?**

In 2018, one animal welfare group helped more than 21,000 animals.

# FOCUS ON
# Animal Rescues

*Write your answers on a separate piece of paper.*

1. Write a letter to a friend describing what you learned about the oil spill in the Gulf of Mexico.

2. If you were an animal rescuer, would you rescue pets or wildlife? Why?

3. In Chapter 1, what did rescue workers use to clean oil off the pelicans?
   - **A.** ocean water
   - **B.** dish soap
   - **C.** refuges

4. Why did the mayor of Mexico City let people bring their pets with them to the shelters?
   - **A.** So the pets could stay with their families.
   - **B.** The shelters were nicer for pets than homes.
   - **C.** The shelters were built mainly for pets to stay in.

**5.** What does the word **inhale** mean in this book?

*During a fire, an animal may **inhale** too much smoke. Rescuers put a mask over the animal's nose. The mask helps the animal breathe.*

    **A.** to move through a fire

    **B.** to blow smoke away

    **C.** to take air into the body

**6.** What does the word **debris** mean in this book?

*Animals were trapped under the rubble. They needed help. Workers discovered the animals while clearing away **debris**.*

    **A.** workers who help animals

    **B.** fences that block an entrance

    **C.** pieces of something that fell apart

*Answer key on page 32.*

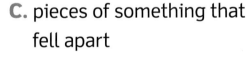

# Glossary

**behavior**
The way a person or animal acts.

**conservation**
The careful protection of plants, animals, and natural resources so they are not lost or wasted.

**CPR**
A way of saving a person or animal whose heartbeat or breathing has stopped.

**harnesses**
Pieces of equipment that hold things in place.

**oil rig**
A machine that takes oil out of the ground.

**ram**
A heavy tool that is used to knock down doors.

**refuges**
Areas that offer safety and shelter.

**veterinarian**
A doctor who treats the injuries and diseases of animals.

**volunteers**
People who help without being paid.

**welfare**
Help given to people or animals in need.

# To Learn More

## BOOKS

Andrus, Aubre. *Animal Rescue.* New York: Scholastic, 2018.

Hunt, Jilly. *Saving Endangered Animals.* Chicago: Capstone, 2018.

Maynard, Thane. *Saving Fiona: The Story of the World's Most Famous Baby Hippo.* Boston: Houghton Mifflin Harcourt, 2018.

## NOTE TO EDUCATORS

Visit **www.focusreaders.com** to find lesson plans, activities, links, and other resources related to this title.

# Index

## B
brown pelicans, 6, 8

## C
conservation groups, 14, 16
CPR, 12

## F
falcons, 15
firefighters, 11, 27

## H
harnesses, 14
headlamps, 22, 26

## K
kayaks, 7

## L
leashes, 22

## P
police officers, 16, 27

## R
rabbits, 18
rams, 22
refuges, 8, 25–26
rescue glides, 13–14

## S
sea turtles, 6
shelters, 7–8, 18, 25
shovels, 24
soldiers, 11, 27

## V
veterinarians, 16

## W
welfare groups, 12, 26, 27

**Answer Key: 1.** Answers will vary; **2.** Answers will vary; **3.** B; **4.** A; **5.** C; **6.** C